United Arab Emirates
─────── The First 30 Years ───────

Published with the support of

United Arab Emirates

——— The First 30 Years ———

A collection of historical photographs by Ramesh Shukla

MOTIVATE
PUBLISHING

Published by Motivate Publishing

Dubai: PO Box 2331, Dubai, UAE
Tel: (+971 4) 282 4060, fax: (+971 4) 282 0428
e-mail: books@motivate.ae   www.booksarabia.com

Office 508, Building No 8, Dubai Media City, Dubai, UAE
Tel: (+971 4) 390 3550, fax: (+971 4) 390 4845

Abu Dhabi: PO Box 43072, Abu Dhabi, UAE
Tel: (+971 2) 677 2005, fax: (+971 2) 677 0124

London: Acre House, 11/15 William Road, London NW1 3ER
e-mail: motivateuk@motivate.ae

Directors:	Obaid Humaid Al Tayer and Ian Fairservice

Consultant Editor:	David Steele
Deputy Editor:	Moushumi Nandy
Assistant Editor:	Zelda Pinto
Art Director:	Andrea Willmore
Designer:	Cithadel Francisco

General Manager Books:	Jonathan Griffiths
Publishing & Rights Coordinator:	Jenny Bateman

First published 2002 by Motivate Publishing
Reprinted 2005, 2007

© Ramesh Shukla and Motivate Publishing 2002

ISBN: 978 1 86063 130 6

British Library Cataloguing-in-Publication Data. A catalogue record for
this book is available from the British Library.

While every care has been taken to accurately caption the
photographs in this book, the dating of some is only approximate.
Historic events have been thoroughly researched, while city scenes
and portraits are intended to capture the essence of an era. The
publishers would be pleased to hear from readers able to provide
further details for inclusion in future editions.

Contents

1960s

and the pre-Federation years

Back in 1968, sailing dhows could still be seen along Dubai's Creek – a waterway which divides the city into two distinct areas, Deira and Bur Dubai.

1960s and the pre-Federation years

As the 1960s dawned, the first indications of modern development were apparent in the seven sheikhdoms that now comprise the United Arab Emirates, then known as the Trucial States.

It's possible to trace the history of these sheikhdoms back more than 7,000 years, thanks to the results of archaeological research in recent decades. Before Federation, the seven – Abu Dhabi, Dubai, Sharjah, Ra's al-Khaimah, Fujairah, Ajman and Umm al-Qaiwain – were known as the Trucial States. Since 1820, the Rulers had been in treaty relations with Britain, under the terms of agreements which preserved their individual sovereignty but gave London the right to handle issues of foreign affairs and defence. Meeting regularly within the framework of the Trucial States Council, established in the early 1950s, the Rulers were already beginning to move towards closer cooperation, although the establishment of a formal Federation was several years off.

The local economy, too, was in a state of transition. The pearling industry, which had been a mainstay of the economy for thousands of years, had come to an end shortly after the Second World War, mainly because of the advent of the Japanese cultured pearl. Dubai, long a centre of maritime trade, was already expanding its commercial links, with new facilities for shipping being provided by the dredging of the Creek. The rudiments of a modern infrastructure, including the first airport and roads and the introduction of electricity, had also begun. In most of the rest of the sheikhdoms, however, either little had changed for centuries, or the devastating effects of the end of the pearling industry were still being felt.

The introduction of modern education had only just started, health facilities were confined to the main towns and most of the people still lived in traditional housing, without access to electricity or regular water supplies. The source of employment for many was simple agriculture in desert oases or the mountain wadis (valleys), while in Abu Dhabi's desert regions, the ancient nomadic lifestyle remained unchanged.

There were already signs, however, of better times to come. The first commercially-viable oilfields had been found in Abu Dhabi, first offshore and then onshore, in 1960. Development had quickly got under way, with the first half of the decade laying the foundations for the growth that was to follow. Oil production began in Abu Dhabi in 1962 and, with the consequent dramatic increase in revenues, the building of infrastructure began, including work on the first proper road links between Abu Dhabi and the rest of the country. In Dubai, too, the search for oil began offshore, meeting with success several years later.

By the mid-1960s, rising oil income in Abu Dhabi, and the related demand from the people that it should be used for the benefit of all, led to a change in leadership that was to prove of unparalleled importance in the development of the country. On August 6, 1966, Sheikh Zayed bin Sultan Al Nahyan was chosen by Abu Dhabi's ruling Al Nahyan family to take over as Ruler.

As the Ruler's Representative in Abu Dhabi's Eastern Region, based in Al Ain since 1946, and the younger brother of Sheikh Shakhbut (who had ruled Abu Dhabi since 1928), Sheikh Zayed had developed a clear vision of how he wished the oil revenues to be used. To this end, he immediately launched a massive development programme, not only funding projects in Abu Dhabi, but elsewhere in the Trucial States.

His generosity yielded dividends when, in early 1968, Britain informed the seven Rulers that they would be pulling out of the Arabian Gulf by the end of 1971. Sheikh Zayed and his fellow Ruler, Sheikh Rashid bin Saeed Al Maktoum of Dubai, immediately recognised that closer links needed to be established between the emirates.

With conflict elsewhere in the region, international observers gave the new state little chance of survival. However, the shared language, history, heritage and beliefs of the people of the seven emirates were to prove far stronger than the observers could have imagined.

A view across Deira, 1969. The Clock Tower, built earlier in the decade, is now surrounded by tall buildings and a major landmark in Dubai, while there's also much more traffic. The Phillips Building is clearly visible behind the Clock Tower; it's since been renovated and is now known as the Embassy Suites.

Left top: A 1968 photograph of the old Dubai–Sharjah Road. In those days the only taxis were Land Rovers.

Left bottom: Abu Dhabi Corniche in the 1960s; this picture was taken from where the fountain now stands. Today, Marina Mall would be visible from this spot, across the water on the right.

Above: Collecting water from a well in Dibba in 1968, when donkeys were used to transport water between wells and homes. Today, Dibba has a large mineral-water bottling plant.

Above: An elderly man rests in front of Ramesh Shukla's former house in Nasser Square, near the old livestock market.

Left: Dancers outside an 'arish (also known as barasti *– both words mean 'palm-frond') house in Satwa, wearing shell skirts that rattle as they move, providing a rhythmic accompaniment to the musical instruments. The large instrument in the centre is a* tamboura.

Previous spread: Following a day at the camel races in 1968, His Highness Sheikh Zayed bin Sultan Al Nahyan and Sheikh Mohammed bin Khalifa Al Nahyan are accompanied by Mohammed Saeed Al Ghaith (centre), Ozair Suroor (in uniform) and other dignitaries on an evening tour of Sharjah.

Following spread: Dubai Creek in the 1960s. Al Ahmadiya School, now renovated as a tourist attraction, was still open at the time and is visible just right and below the centre of the picture, in Deira.

1970s

A new beginning

Sheikh Zayed signs the Federation Agreement on December 2, 1971, giving birth to the United Arab Emirates. On his left is Sheikh Rashid, then Ruler of Dubai. Behind them are Mehdi Al Tajir, Sheikh Maktoum bin Rashid and Sheikh Hamdan bin Rashid.

1970s – A new beginning

With the final withdrawal of the British from the Gulf looming, Sheikh Zayed of Abu Dhabi and Sheikh Rashid of Dubai took the initiative to bring together the Rulers of the seven emirates in a series of meetings. First agreeing to federate their own states, they invited the other five emirates, as well as nearby Qatar and Bahrain, to join. The response was quick and favourable.

Qatar and Bahrain finally decided to opt for a separate international status, but the Rulers of the seven Trucial States endorsed the concept of the Federation of the United Arab Emirates, which formally took its place in the international community on December 2, 1971. At the outset there were six members, with Ra's al-Khaimah, the seventh, joining a couple of months later. Sheikh Zayed was elected the first President, a post to which he has been re-elected at successive five-year intervals, while Sheikh Rashid was elected Vice-President, a post he held until his death in 1990.

The new UAE had an inauspicious beginning, thanks to the seizure of the islands of Abu Musa and Greater and Lesser Tunb by Iran and a dispute over the common border with Saudi Arabia. Internally, strife in Sharjah just after the UAE was established led to a change of Ruler. Moreover, with oil revenues already flowing into Abu Dhabi and Dubai, these two emirates had begun a development programme that was rapidly widening the gap between them and the other members of the Federation.

From the outset, however, Sheikh Zayed and Sheikh Rashid displayed their determination to ensure expenditure on development was spread as evenly as possible throughout the Federation. A major programme of building the necessary infrastructure, such as roads, housing and water and electricity utilities was set in motion, while substantial investment was also made in the expansion of education and health services, which in many areas had been rudimentary or even non-existent.

Expanding oil production, particularly in Abu Dhabi, provided additional revenues, while the massive increase in oil prices that followed the 1973 October War between the Arabs and Israel played its part in the transformation of the United Arab Emirates from a relatively poor country into a state with one of the highest per-capita incomes in the world.

Unlike many other countries, the UAE could afford to pay for the development of its infrastructure and the only restraint on the programme was simply that it took time for the projects to be completed. Gradually, however, the features of the modern state began to appear.

With the introduction of state-wide compulsory free education, illiteracy rates began to fall sharply, while the country's first university was opened in the inland oasis-city of Al Ain in 1978. As the health services expanded, there was a parallel decline in the incidence of disease and life expectancy began to rise, a process that today has put the UAE on a par with the world's most advanced states.

A modern system of highways was built, first linking the major towns and then beginning to spread out through the more remote desert areas, to ensure that the benefits of the development programme were taken to the people.

Old housing, of blocks of stone or coral, or of date-palm fronds ('arish) was replaced with modern buildings, many built at Government expense and then given, without charge, to the country's citizens. In major population centres, architectural and landscaping features such as the Abu Dhabi Corniche and Dubai Creek began to take on their present shape, lined with modern buildings, although progress could also be noted in smaller towns such as Ra's al-Khaimah and Fujairah.

Out in the desert, as well as in the cities, a massive programme of afforestation got under way with the planting of millions of trees, part of a dream to 'make the desert green'; now, a couple of decades later, the UAE is one of the greenest countries in Arabia.

Another feature of the 1970s was the emergence of the UAE as a major transhipment and trading centre for the region, taking advantage of its geographical location between East and West. Both sea ports and airports in the country benefited from this process and, by the end of the decade, the country derived much of its income from commercial traffic, continuing a tradition of maritime trade that stretches back more than 7,000 years.

Leader in the field, thanks to the visionary commercial acumen of Sheikh Rashid, was Dubai. With Port Rashid quickly established as a major port, construction of the port at Jebel Ali, one of the largest man-made structures in the world, and one of the few that can be seen from space, began.

All this progress took place against a background of the steady consolidation of the Federation. The currency and the postal system were unified, a common flag was adopted and, later in the decade, the Rulers took the important decision to unify the armed forces. In 1976, as the UAE completed its first five years, Sheikh Zayed and Sheikh Rashid were re-elected to continue the process of national transformation.

By the end of the decade, the fledgling state had not only shown its durability and envied internal stability, but had also earned considerable recognition and respect overseas. Through its principled foreign policy as well as the cautious and consistent approach adopted in relation to its role as a key member of the Organisation of Petroleum Exporting Countries, Opec, it had also become a voice to be reckoned with at a regional level.

Underlying it all, of course, was not only the UAE's good fortune in terms of its oil reserves, but also the fact that its leaders, above all Sheikh Zayed and Sheikh Rashid, were blessed with the vision and intuition to see what could be achieved, and the determination to ensure that the dreams came true.

Bin Yas Street opposite The Carlton Tower Hotel, Dubai, 1970s. 'Bin Yas' means 'the son of Yas'; Yas was the legendary founder of the Bani Yas, one of the earliest tribes to settle in the region. It's the main tribe in both Abu Dhabi and Dubai and the tribe of which the rulers of both emirates are members.

Above: The Bin Rashid Al Maktoum brothers: Sheikh Maktoum, Vice President and Prime Minister of the UAE and current Ruler of Dubai; Sheikh Hamdan, Deputy Ruler of Dubai and Minister of Finance and Industry; and Sheikh Mohammed, Crown Prince of Dubai and Minister of Defence; at Union House (also known as Dar Al Ittihad) on Federation Day, December 2, 1971.

Right top: Sheikh Zayed with Ahmed bin Khalifa Al Suwaidi, the first Foreign Minister of the UAE, at the Federation table. To the right is Ahmed bin Sulayem and to the far left is the late General Hamouda bin Ali, former Minister of State for the Interior.

Right bottom: Celebrations taking place behind Union House after the signing of the Federation Agreement and the raising of the first national flag. In the foreground on the right is Sheikh Rashid with Easa Saleh Al Gurg, current UAE Ambassador to the UK.

Above: An historic moment under the new flag. From left to right are Sheikh Khalid bin Mohammed Al Qasimi, then Ruler of Sharjah; Sheikh Rashid bin Saeed Al Maktoum, then Vice-President of the UAE and Ruler of Dubai; Sheikh Zayed bin Sultan Al Nahyan, President of the UAE and Ruler of Abu Dhabi; Sheikh Rashid bin Humaid Al Nuaimi, then Ruler of Ajman; Sheikh Mohammed bin Hamad Al Sharqi, then Ruler of Fujairah; and Sheikh Rashid bin Ahmed Al Mualla, then Crown Prince, now Ruler, of

Umm al-Qaiwain. Although he attended the Federation meetings, Sheikh Saqr bin Mohammed Al Qasimi, Ruler of Ra's al-Khaimah, initially opted not to sign the agreement. Nevertheless, the emirate joined the United Arab Emirates in February the following year.

Right: Some Abu Dhabi children find a novel way to get a good view of the first National Day anniversary celebrations on December 2, 1972.

*Above: Sheikh Zayed and Sheikh Rashid, the architects of the
Federation, in earnest discussion at Za'abeel Palace, 1971.*

*Right: Sheikh Zayed reads an official document received from
Sultan Qaboos of Oman.*

Above: Sheikh Mohammed bin Rashid makes a speech at the opening ceremony for Port Rashid in Dubai, 1975. The new port was to have a major impact on Dubai's economy.

Right: The former Ruler of Ajman, Sheikh Rashid bin Humaid Al Nuaimi, with Indian Ambassador, Mr Razvi, in Ajman Palace in the mid-70s. Sheikh Rashid was Ruler of Ajman from 1928 until his death in 1981.

Right: Sheikh Rashid bin Ahmed Al Mualla, present Ruler of Umm al-Qaiwain, with Khalifa Al Nabooda, former Undersecretary of the Ministry of Defence and now a leading businessman in Dubai, 1972.

Below: Dr Sheikh Sultan bin Mohammed Al Qasimi, the present Ruler of Sharjah, and Sheikh Humaid bin Rashid Al Nuaimi, then Crown Prince, now Ruler of Ajman, during a visit to Sheikh Rashid in Dubai.

Far right: Sheikh Rashid with Sheikh Ahmed bin Ali Al Thani of Qatar (on extreme right of photo). Standing sideways between them is Ahmed Al Moosa, Treasurer and Financial Controller. Sheikh Ahmed was Ruler of Qatar from 1960 to 1972.

Right: The funeral of Sheikh Khalid bin Mohammed Al Qasimi, former Ruler of Sharjah.

Below: Rain falls during the funeral of the wife of Sheikh Rashid bin Saeed Al Maktoum. Sheikh Mohammed and Sheikh Hamdan can be seen leading the many mourners.

Far right: Sheikh Rashid inspects the workings of a petroleum installation with Mehdi Al Tajir, former Ambassador to the UK, in 1976.

*Above: At the opening of the terminal at Dubai Airport in 1970
are Sheikh Rashid bin Humaid Al Nuaimi of Ajman and Sheikh
Khalifa bin Zayed Al Nahyan, Crown Prince of Abu Dhabi.*

*Right top: Two of Dubai's leading businessmen, Juma Al Majid
and Saif Al Ghurair, in discussion outside the venue of the Middle
East Construction Exhibition in 1977.*

*Right bottom: Members of the Dubai Chamber of Commerce at the
last meeting in their former building in 1978. Pictured from left to
right are Hamad Al Futtaim, Khalaf Al Habtoor, Majid Al
Futtaim and Sheikh Hasher bin Maktoum Al Maktoum.*

Above: Sheikh Rashid inspects plans with Khalaf Al Habtoor while touring the new Dubai Petroleum Companies office in Jumeirah.

Left: Sheikh Rashid turns the first spadeful of sand at the groundbreaking ceremony of the Dubai Petroleum Companies office, 1975.

Above: Maqta Bridge, 1972. Construction of the bridge was completed in 1968, giving the island of Abu Dhabi a permanent link to the mainland.

Left: The transformation of Abu Dhabi from a small town to a thriving city took just 20 years. This road was known as Television Road in the 70s and is now situated in the heart of the city's commercial district.

Above: Sunset over Dubai Creek, captured from Deira.

Right top: During the 70s, water buffalo visited Hamriya daily to bathe. Although the buffalo may have disappeared, you can still see dhows being constructed alongside Dubai's Creek today.

Right bottom: Unloading timber from dhows in Dubai Creek, 1972. The timber was used in the construction of buildings and dhows and for manufacturing furniture.

Above: The Jashanmal & Sons shop used to stand in the area where Nasser Square is today. The Jashanmals set up this store in 1956 when the elder brother, Atma, came to Dubai from Bahrain. The square was named after Gamal Abdul Nasser, the Egyptian leader of the Arab League who died in 1970.

Left top: The first Chamber of Commerce exhibition took place in 1975 on the site where the Twin Towers now stand. The old Customs Houses can be seen on the opposite bank of the Creek.

Left bottom: A view across the roofs of Bur Dubai in the area near the Ambassador Hotel – one of the first hotels built in Dubai.

Right: Fakhruddin Ali Ahmed, President of India, visited Dubai in 1976. Among the dignitaries to meet him were Hiro Jashanmal (second from right).

Below: A view of the terminal at Dubai's new airport, which opened in 1971.

Far right top: A group of men make repairs to a dhow in Sharjah. Note the sailing dhows in the background; sadly, these have since all but disappeared from the waters of the Gulf.

Far right bottom: Construction of a high-rise tower under way in Sharjah, 1971.

One of the old watch-towers that overlook Hatta village,
photographed in 1978. Today a major tarmac road runs at the base
of the hill and Hatta Heritage Village is across the road.

Traditional fishing boats in Khor Fakkan, 1972. The area is still a fishing centre but the boats have been replaced by fibreglass craft with powerful outboard engines.

Above: Guests arrive at a 1970's wedding in Khor Fakkan, holding flags in celebration.

Right: A young Khor Fakkan fisherman proudly displays his catch.

Above: Much of the elegant architecture of old Dubai has been retained in Bastakiya, the former merchant area on the southern side of the Creek. This is what it looked like in the 70s – current renovation work should soon restore it to its former glory.

Left: A traditional door photographed in Bastakiya in 1975.

Above: Dubai Museum opened its doors to the public in 1971; most appropriately, it was established in Al Fahidi Fort, itself an important part of Dubai's history. Here, repairs are being made to a traditional boat on display.

Left: Intriguing displays of traditional ways of life – and of transport – can be seen in the museum.

*Above: Young children playing in the sand behind Passport Road in
Abu Dhabi in 1972.*

*Right: A cat looks on with great interest as a fisherman cleans his
catch aboard a dhow in Dubai Creek in the early 1970s.*

Right: A falcon perches on its wakir. *Among the traditional pastimes still practiced in the UAE is falconry, a popular sport that provides a unique partnership between man and raptor.*

Below: Sheikh Mohammed bin Rashid leads an impressive line-up of camels during Sheikh Maktoum's wedding celebrations in 1970.

Far right: Traditional drummers at the same wedding.

Following spread: One of the earliest meetings of the Indian Association of Dubai, in the early 1970s. The meetings were attended by prominent businessmen such as Hiro Jashanmal, founder of Jashanmal National Company LLC (on the extreme left, second row from the bottom of the photograph) and Vasu Shroff, owner of Regal Traders (to his left).

Above: A rare portrait of a farmer's wife and a goat taken at a farm in Fujairah in the 70s.

Right: A construction worker taking a break in Deira in 1970.

1980s

The growth continues

Contrasts in architecture: The mosque in the Ruler's Diwan complex and a wind-tower framed by foliage.

1980s – The growth continues

As the United Arab Emirates approached the beginning of its second decade, the political and social stability which had been so evident in its early years was to prove of particular importance. Political upheaval in its neighbour across the Arabian Gulf, Iran, in 1979 was followed by military conflict between Iran and Iraq for most of the decade, posing unforeseen difficulties for the continued development of the UAE's international trade. Another unwelcome development was a sudden and sharp decline in international oil prices, which reflected adversely on Government revenues as well as the ability to press ahead with the consolidation and completion of the state's infrastructure.

At a regional level, the UAE took the initiative to bring together like-minded states in the rest of the Arabian Peninsula and, in May 1981, the six-member Arab Gulf Co-operation Council, AGCC, was founded at a summit conference in Abu Dhabi. Comprising Kuwait, Saudi Arabia, Bahrain, Qatar and Oman, as well as the Emirates, this body drew, in part, on the successful experiment of federation in the UAE. It also provided a framework through which collaboration could be developed, both for tackling internal issues of development and for strengthening the ability of the UAE and its fellow AGCC members to deal with the challenges posed by insecurity in the area.

Internally, thanks to the leadership of President Sheikh Zayed and Vice-President Sheikh Rashid, who had also become Prime Minister in 1979, the development programme continued almost unabated. Much of the decade was, in fact, a time of consolidation. With the infrastructure more or less complete in the major urban centres (although the rapidly-growing population necessitated continued large-scale development), modern facilities were extended into the smaller settlements, particularly in the Hajar Mountains. By the end of the decade, virtually every hamlet and mountain farm had been connected to the electricity- and water-supply grid, and access to education and health services was available to all.

Although oil revenues continued to flow in, thanks partly to the expansion of production capacity in Abu Dhabi, which held more than 90 per cent of the country's total reserves, a sharp lesson was learned from the sudden collapse of oil prices early in the decade, and special attention was paid to the development of a non-oil industrial sector. Leading the way was Dubai, where the completion of Port Jebel Ali was followed by the establishment of the massive Dubal aluminium smelter and other industrial plants. Abu Dhabi, too, played its part, in particular through the construction of downstream oil ventures such as the Ruwais refinery, and through the harnessing for liquefaction and export of the associated gas reserves in the oilfields, which had formerly been flared.

Another feature of the economic-diversification programme was the first hesitant steps towards creating a tourist industry. Shrewd hoteliers recognised that the UAE, with its long and unspoilt beaches, mountains and deserts, and its attractive Bedu heritage, coupled with an economic environment that permitted tax-free bargains, offered an unusual and diverse combination of attractions for foreign visitors. With the support of Government, particularly in the Northern Emirates, the industry slowly grew.

At the same time, the decision was taken to begin promoting the UAE as a centre for world-class sport. The first proper grass golf courses were built and a host of other sporting events, such as tennis and cricket, helped to attract visitors. Responding to the opportunity thus created, the UAE's own airline, Emirates, was established.

Oil revenues continued to provide the greater part of the Gross Domestic Product, GDP, but through the course of the 1980s, the contribution of the non-oil sector gradually began to increase, although it did not overtake oil until the 1990s.

The consolidation of the state, and its increasing maturity as a significant player in the region, also meant that a growing number of international statesmen and politicians, such as India's Prime Minister Indira Gandhi and King Fahd of Saudi Arabia, made their way to the UAE.

Growing prosperity set in train a process of continued construction. In the major cities, smaller buildings from the 1960s and 70s were often torn down, to be replaced by modern skyscrapers. At the same time, however, attention was paid to preserving the country's national heritage. In the words of President Sheikh Zayed, "A people that does not know its past can understand neither the present nor the future."

With Government support, traditional sports such as camel-racing and boat-racing were revitalised, while the ancient Arab sport of falconry took on a new lease of life with the introduction of modern techniques such as radio-tagging of birds to ensure they did not get lost while hunting.

Despite the frenetic construction, some of the finer examples of old buildings, such as Al Fahidi Fort in Dubai and castles and forts in the other Emirates, were preserved, not only ensuring that evidence remained of past ways, but also providing additional attractions for the tourist industry.

Amid all this, the process of expansion of community services continued. New roads, schools, hospitals and houses were built, the ports and airports were expanded, and the UAE's telecommunications provider, Etisalat, ensured that the country was equipped with the best available in terms of communications links.

Dubai International Airport's first duty-free complex opened in 1983 and the Dubai-based Emirates airline started operations in 1985. Both organisations were to enjoy spectacular growth and become leaders in their field.

Enjoying stability throughout the 1980s, the UAE completed the decade as one of the most successful states in the region, evidence of the wisdom of its founders and the determination with which they had set about building the Federation.

Old and new: The modern façade of The Continental Hotel in Sharjah, under construction, contrasts with a dhow propped up for repair.

Two views across Dubai Creek, 1982, clearly showing the contrast between the old buildings of Bastakiya and the new high-rise developments of Deira.

Right: The changing face of Dubai: Deira Tower at Nasser Square, 1984.

Below: Dubai Creek, 1983, and another view of the modern buildings featured on the previous spread.

Right top: Workers clean up the Creek at Ras al-Khor and plant mangroves in preparation for a site that's now an important conservation area. Mangroves prevent silting and erosion and provide a breeding ground for various aquatic animals.

Right bottom: A cargo of timber (a traditional import) offloaded at Hamriya in 1983.

Above: A wind-tower in Bastakiya. Introduced from Iran, wind-towers were an early form of air-conditioning, trapping the wind or breeze and directing it down to the interior of the building.

Left: A group of tourists enjoying an excellent example of traditional architecture in Bastakiya in 1985. Ramesh Shukla's gallery was housed in this building at the time.

Above: Fishing boats depart from Abu Dhabi near the spot where the new Marina Mall now stands.

Left top and bottom: Scenes from the Abu Dhabi Corniche area in the 1980s, showing the continuing growth of the city.

Previous spread: Races with rowing boats – as well as with graceful sailing dhows – are regularly held off Abu Dhabi and other centres.

Left: By 1980, Sharjah was attracting an increasing and varied amount of shipping.

Below: Sharjah's Central Souk, also known as the Blue Souk, was opened in 1978 on the northern shore of Khalid Lagoon, opposite Jazira Park. The souk is cooled by natural means, with the high entrances and wind-towers channelling breezes inside the buildings.

Far left top: Some examples of traditional architecture still survived in Sharjah in 1986. Sadly, as in other cities around the world, many have since disappeared, although a few finer buildings have been preserved.

Far left bottom: Camels and dhows contrast with modern tugs and oil tanks on Sharjah's Waterfront.

Above: While their falcon waits nearby, a hunting group relaxes round their fire in the desert.

Left top, left: Hatta Pools, located in a large, scenic wadi, generally have water all year round and are deep enough to swim in.

Left top right: Portrait of a girl near Ra's al-Khaimah, 1985.

Left bottom: Dunes beside the road between Al Ain and Dubai.

Left: A collection of traditional Arabian coffee pots.

Above: Traders take some welcome refreshment in the area behind Naif Road, Dubai, 1980.

Faces of the UAE: The sand-covered face of a Bedu contrasts with those of two women displaying their traditional dress and jewellery.

Above: Camel races under way in the area behind Dubai World Trade Centre, 1984.

Left: Some youngsters making use of the camel races to test their riding skills.

Above: Royal entertainment at Sheikh Hamdan bin Rashid Al Maktoum's wedding, 1987, with Arabian horses being raced around a UAE flag. The Arabian breed has recently been returned to the peninsula and is extremely popular among local breeders.

Left top: At the camel races at Nad Al Sheba, near Dubai, 1989.

Left bottom: The start of a camel race in Dubai, 1980.

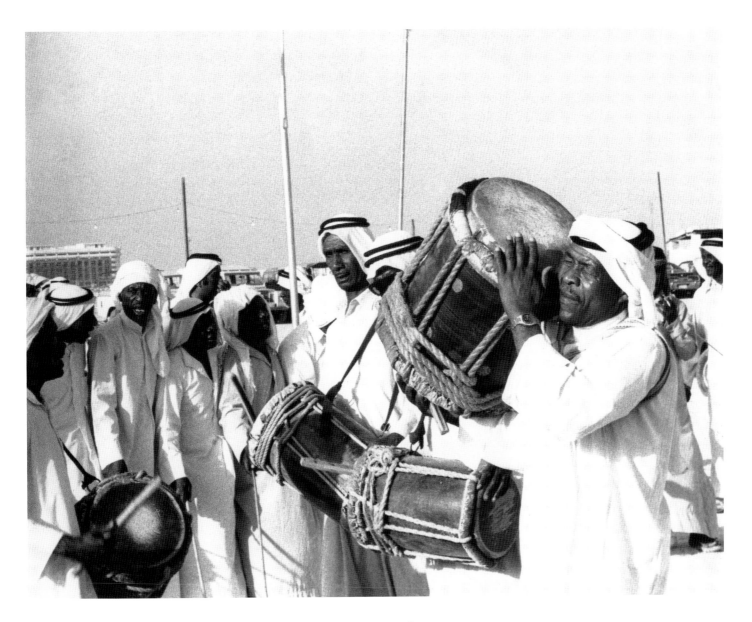

*This page: Traditional music and dancing, such as that pictured
here, forms an important part of wedding celebrations, with the
men and women performing separate dances.*

*Following spread: Guests – all prominent businessmen – at Tayeb
Baker's wedding, 1983. From left to right are Haj Ali Fathallah,
Ali Akbar, Abdullah Qayed, Tayeb Baker (the groom), Tariq
Ahmad Abdulrahim Baker and Salim Mismar.*

Left top: Sheikh Rashid with two of his grandchildren and Dr Mohammed Habib Al Redha at Sheikh Mohammed's wedding, 1980. The two children are Sheikh Saeed bin Maktoum and his sister. Dr Mohammed was the first Arab doctor in Dubai.

Left bottom: Sheikh Hamdan accompanied (on his right) by Mohammed bin Sheikh Mejren and others at the same wedding.

Above: Sheikh Rashid bin Saeed Al Maktoum in 1980.

Above: Sheikh Maktoum greets Easa Saleh Al Gurg, the UAE Ambassador to the UK and the Republic of Ireland, in 1980.

Right top: Sheikh Rashid pictured with Indira Gandhi, Prime Minister of India, during her visit to the UAE.

Right bottom: King Fahd bin Abdul Aziz of Saudi Arabia is welcomed at Dubai Airport by the UAE's seven rulers in 1986.

1990s

and into the new millennium

Fireworks paint the sky, marking the beginning of the annual Dubai Shopping Festival in 2000.

1990s *and into the new millennium*

The beginning of the 1990s saw the Arabian Gulf region once again beset by turmoil, as a result of Iraq's invasion of Kuwait in August, 1990. The United Arab Emirates was closely involved in the international coalition to liberate Kuwait, with the UAE armed forces taking part in both the land battles and the aerial conflict.

There were, though, beneficial side-effects: a demand from Emirati women that they, too, should be permitted to play their part in the defence of the country led to the formation of a special women's unit in the armed forces, the first in the GCC states; while an upsurge of national feeling saw thousands of young – and not-so-young – men volunteering for service. This all had a marked effect on consolidating a feeling of unity among the people of the Emirates.

The autumn of 1990 also brought grief to the country with the death of Sheikh Rashid bin Saeed Al Maktoum who, as Ruler of Dubai, had collaborated closely with President Sheikh Zayed bin Sultan Al Nahyan, Ruler of Abu Dhabi, in creating the Federation and had subsequently served as a distinguished Vice-President for 19 years. He was succeeded as Vice-President, Prime Minister and Ruler of Dubai by his Crown Prince, Sheikh Maktoum bin Rashid Al Maktoum.

In the aftermath of change at home and turmoil further north, it was apparent that, after nearly 20 years of life, the UAE had become a mature and confident state. It was also clear that the programme of diversifying its economy away from dependence on oil and gas was an effective one. Despite the inevitable disruption of patterns of international trade because of the Kuwait conflict, economic development continued to push ahead.

The ports of Khor Fakkan and Fujairah, on the East Coast, saw a surge in business from shipping lines eager to avoid the higher 'war risk' insurance rates in the Gulf, but ports inside the Gulf, in particular Port Rashid and Port Jebel Ali in Dubai, also continued to expand. At Jebel Ali, the nascent free zone succeeded in attracting growing business, part of a process that has

now made it one of the largest zones of its kind in Asia.

In the early 1990s, the UAE resumed the development of its strategic role as the most important transhipment centre in the region. There were consequent benefits for the shipping business, as well as airports and airlines, with Emirates, the national carrier, rapidly introducing new routes as well as winning a succession of international awards.

The strength of the local economy was reflected in the pace of construction, with the skylines of the major cities changing almost weekly as new hotels and office and apartment blocks were built to cater for increasing demand. The tourist industry grew rapidly, with a whole series of new attractions being developed for visitors, particularly in Dubai, which launched a programme of top-class sporting events ranging from tennis and golf to powerboat-racing and horse-racing. By the middle of the decade, the UAE was firmly established as an international sporting venue.

In 1996, the UAE celebrated its Silver Jubilee, the completion of 25 years of existence during which the seven emirates had not only forged a strong Federation, but had also successfully undergone a complete transformation in terms of development. Whereas in 1971 the benefits of modern facilities were still largely confined to the major population centres, by 1996 every member of the population had access to education, health facilities and decent housing. Employment opportunities for all had been created, thanks partly to the rapidly diversifying economy, and modern communications were available in even the most remote areas. In achieving that progress, the lion's share of the credit lay with Sheikh Zayed, whose vision, generosity and determination had made it all possible.

It is not in the nature of the people of the UAE to rest on their laurels. Satisfaction with the achievements of the first 25 years was matched with aspirations to proceed still further and, during the course of the second half of the 1990s, development continued unabated. Imaginative new ventures such as the launch of the annual Dubai Shopping Festival helped to prompt further growth in the tourist industry and this, in turn, created more business for hotels, airlines, airports and shop owners. The result? Further investment in construction.

The 'open door' economic policy followed by the country since 1971 also helped a growing number of international businesses to select the UAE as their regional base, while particular effort was made to ensure that the country remained at the forefront in technological innovation through, for example, the establishment of the Dubai Internet and Media Cities.

As the new millennium dawned, the UAE had consolidated its position as the key centre for international commerce in the region. At the same time, however, and despite the phenomenal pace of development, attention continued to be paid to the preservation and protection of the country's culture and heritage. A country-wide programme of restoring

ancient buildings, such as those in Dubai's Shindagha district, or historic settlements and forts in Sharjah, Ra's al-Khaimah, Umm al-Qaiwain, Ajman, Fujairah, Al Ain and Hatta, served to remind both residents and visitors of the country's past.

The United Arab Emirates has now become one of the world's most modern states, with a highly diversified economy no longer solely dependent on oil and gas, and enjoying the very latest in social services and other facilities. At the same time, it retains the essential nature of its culture. The welcome combination offers both continued prosperity and social and economic stability for many years ahead.

Queen Rania of Jordan and former US President Bill Clinton accompany Sheikh Mohammed to the Stars ceremony in Dubai, 2002.

Left: Young boys wave the UAE flag to celebrate National Day on December 2, 2000.

Below: Sheikh Mohammed bin Rashid at an exhibition to mark the UAE's Silver Jubilee in 1996. Standing next to him, from right to left, are Khalfan Musabeh, Director of the Cultural Foundation in Abu Dhabi; Sheikh Abdullah bin Zayed Al Nahyan, Minister of Information and Culture; and Ahmed Humaid Al Tayer, Minister of Commerce and Industry.

Right: A procession through Dubai during the UAE's colourful Silver Jubilee celebrations.

Above: Sheikh Mohammed bin Rashid at the unveiling of plans for Dubai's Festival City. The multi-phase project will transform the site on Dubai Creek into a world-class destination for dining, shopping and entertainment, and will also feature a mammoth 8,000-seat amphitheatre, offices, residential units and hotels.

Left top: A model of Dubai's Gold and Diamond Park is studied by dignitaries at its opening in May, 2001.

Left bottom: Sheikh Mohammed bin Rashid is interviewed at the opening of Dubai Women's College, 1989.

Above: Young dancers perform at BurJuman Shopping Centre to mark the opening of Dubai Shopping Festival, 2000. The festival has encapsulated the entrepreneurial spirit of the emirate since its inception in 1996 and draws visitors from all over the world.

Left: First held in 1996, the Dubai World Cup is renowned as the world's richest horse-race. These scenes were captured in 2001 (top) and 1999 (bottom).

*Above: Sheikh Hamdan bin Rashid opens a new road tunnel
opposite the World Trade Centre in 1996. To his left is Mohammed
Al Noori of Dubai Municipality.*

*Left: Since it was first held in 1989, the biennial Dubai Air Show
has established itself as the third biggest of its kind in the world,
after the Farnborough and Paris air shows. These scenes were taken
at the 2001 show.*

Above: Visitors at the opening of the National Bank of Dubai building in 1997. The pearl collection of Sultan Ali Al Owais, the largest in the world, can be seen on display around the room.

Left top: At the opening of the renovated Sheikh Saeed Al Maktoum House, now a key tourist attraction, in 1996 are from left to right: Saif Al Ghurair, Sheikh Hamdan bin Rashid Al Maktoum and Sheikh Ahmed bin Saeed Al Maktoum.

Left bottom: Sheikh Ahmed bin Rashid Al Maktoum, Deputy Chairman of Dubai Police and Public Security, with Sheikh Ahmed bin Saeed Al Maktoum, President of the Dubai Department of Civil Aviation and Chairman of Emirates airline, and the young Sheikh Maktoum bin Hamdan Al Maktoum.

Rulers and dignitaries at the opening of Burj Al Arab (Tower of the Arabs), the world's tallest hotel when it opened in 1999. In the foreground, from the left are: Sheikh Saqr bin Mohammed Al Qasimi, Ruler of R'as al-Khaimah; Sheikh Humaid bin Rashid Al Nuaimi, Ruler of Ajman; Sheikh Rashid bin Ahmed Al Mualla, Ruler of Umm al-Qaiwain and Sheikh Hamad bin Saif Al Sharqi, Deputy Ruler of Fujairah.

Left: The 202-suite hotel, which is floodlit at night, was built on its own man-made island and stands 321 metres high.

Right: The restored Ajman Fort – the former residence of the Ruler of Ajman – dates back to approximately 1775 and now houses the Ajman Museum.

Below: Ajman is the smallest of the emirates and its main territory is bordered by Sharjah. The town has the largest dhow-building yard in the UAE.

Hatta Fort has undergone extensive renovations and re-opened in 2001 as the centrepiece of the Hatta Heritage Village. The distinctive watch-towers on the hills overlooking the fort protected the inhabitants dwelling below. (A photograph of one of the watch-towers as it looked before restoration appears on page 48.)

Above: Reputed to be 360 years old, Fujairah Fort was damaged in the early 20th century by a British bombardment. It has recently been restored and is to become a museum.

Left: It's with good reason that Al Ain is known as the Oasis City.

Etisalat, the Emirates Telecommunications Corporation, established in 1976, is 60-per-cent state-owned and 40-per-cent owned by private UAE investors. Etisalat has become one of the most profitable telecommunications organisations in the Middle East. Pictured here are the Etisalat buildings in Fujairah (above) and Sharjah (right).

Left: One of the most attractive areas in Abu Dhabi is the Corniche, shown here in 1990.

Below left and right: As is the case in most cities, Abu Dhabi is constantly growing and – despite the city's relatively young age – some of the older buildings are already making way for the new. These buildings are typical of those found in the Corniche area in the 1990s.

Far left: The Al Qasbah area is one of the latest developments in Sharjah and incorporates the Qasbah Mosque (which has English-language services) and the Qasbah Canal, which has a promenade alongside.

Different views of the Abu Dhabi Corniche area. The headquarters of a number of major oil companies and leading banks are situated here.

Above: Sheikh Zayed Road is the new ultra-high-rise central business district of Dubai, where each new tower fronting the road seems more modern and striking than the last.

Right top: The futuristic skyline of Sheikh Zayed Road seen from the nature reserve at Ra's al-Khor. When compared with the picture on page 71, the development of the reserve and of Sheikh Zayed Road are staggering.

Right bottom: The golden reflections of the Creek on the curved frontage of The National Bank of Dubai building are nothing short of eye-catching, especially in the late afternoon. The innovative architecture of the surrounding Chamber of Commerce, Sheraton and Etisalat buildings ensure that this is one of the most photographed scenes in Dubai.

Above: Old buildings and wind-towers still stood in Bur Dubai in the 1990s; across the Creek, development was more conspicuous.

Right top: Young children attend a traditional Quran class at Dubai Heritage Village.

Right bottom: Eid prayers being held at Eidgah, near the World Trade Centre, in 2001.

Groups of people regularly gather at Dubai Heritage Village to recreate the old Arabian way of life and to keep traditional skills and crafts alive. Here, in 2001, traditional methods of obtaining and transporting water, and ways of cooking, are demonstrated.

Traditional dance and music is very much alive today and regularly performed by groups during festivals and celebrations, providing an ideal opportunity for residents and visitors to learn more about the cultural heritage of the UAE.

Despite all the changes since the discovery of oil – or perhaps because of them – the people of the UAE proudly maintain their traditions and nowhere is this more apparent than in their dress. It's also interesting to note the differences in dress between the women of the cities and of the rural areas; for visitors with little time, an outing to Dubai Heritage Village should provide some colourful examples.

Above: One of the traditional skills being kept alive – and passed on to the younger generation – at the Heritage Village is the weaving of fishing nets (above).

*Right: Abdullah Hamdan, manager of Dubai Heritage Village, looks on as a palm-frond (*barasti *or* 'arish) *hut is constructed.*

Everyday scenes in the Heritage Village provide the visitor with a unique glimpse into the Arabian way of life – and some wonderful photographic opportunities.

Above: Noses are rubbed together in a traditional greeting.

Left top: After a long day of fasting during Ramadan, a group of UAE citizens enjoy iftar *(a light meal used to break the fast).*

Left bottom: Sheikh Saeed Al Maktoum House, situated near the mouth of the Creek, was the evocative venue for an awards ceremony of the Dubai Shopping Festival.

Following spread: Hamad bin Rahma Al Shamsi, whose father was a leading pearl merchant, weighing pearls in traditional hand-held scales (left) and Abdulla Jaber, a leading Dubai businessman, pictured at one of his stores (right).

Above: A young boy relaxes on the mats and carpets on sale in his father's store in the Shindagha area of Dubai.

Left: Sara A Rahman, a well-known local artist, at work.

Acknowledgements

I would like to thank the following for their support and inspiration:

The Rulers of the United Arab Emirates
For their foresight and wisdom and for allowing me the opportunity to photograph them over the years.

Jashanmal National Company
With special acknowledgement to Hiro Jashanmal and Gangu Batra. I am forever indebted to Hiro Jashanmal, the company's founder who guided and supported me when I first arrived in Dubai.

Motivate Publishing
With special mention to Ian Fairservice, Managing Partner
and Alison Ashbee, Johnson Machado, Jackie Nel, Simon O'Herlihy and David Steele.

And my family
Taru, Neel and Sylvia, for their continued love and support.

HH Sheikh Zayed bin Sultan Al Nahyan with Ramesh Shukla in 1968.

HH Sheikh Maktoum bin Rashid Al Maktoum greets Ramesh Shukla, 1998.

The late Hiro Jashanmal and Ramesh Shukla at the launch of Shukla's first book.

The publishers are grateful to their friends at Jashanmal, who have been trading in the UAE since 1956 and have shared the excitement of producing this book. It would not have been possible without their support and encouragement.

JASHANMAL
National Company L.L.C.